KU-463-855

how to live a
kind
life

how to live a
kind
life

ONE HUNDRED WAYS TO
A PEACEFUL LIFE

B **Bounty**
BOOKS

An Hachette UK Company
www.hachette.co.uk

First published as *Everyday Kindness* in 2017
by Bounty Books,
a division of Octopus Publishing Group Ltd
Carmelite House
50 Victoria Embankment
London, EC4Y 0DZ

Published in 2018 by Bounty Books, a division of
Octopus Publishing Group Ltd

www.octopusbooks.co.uk

Copyright © Octopus Publishing Group Ltd 2017,
2018

All rights reserved. No part of this work may
be reproduced or utilized in any form or by
any means, electronic or mechanical, including
photocopying, recording or by any information
storage and retrieval system, without the prior
written permission of the publisher.

ISBN: 978-0-7537-3282-3

A CIP catalogue record for this book is available
from the British Library

Printed and bound in China

10 9 8 7 6 5 4 3 2 1

Publisher: Lucy Pessell
Designer: Lisa Layton
Editor: Sarah Vaughan
Production Controller: Beata Kibil
Images: Shutterstock/Irtsya

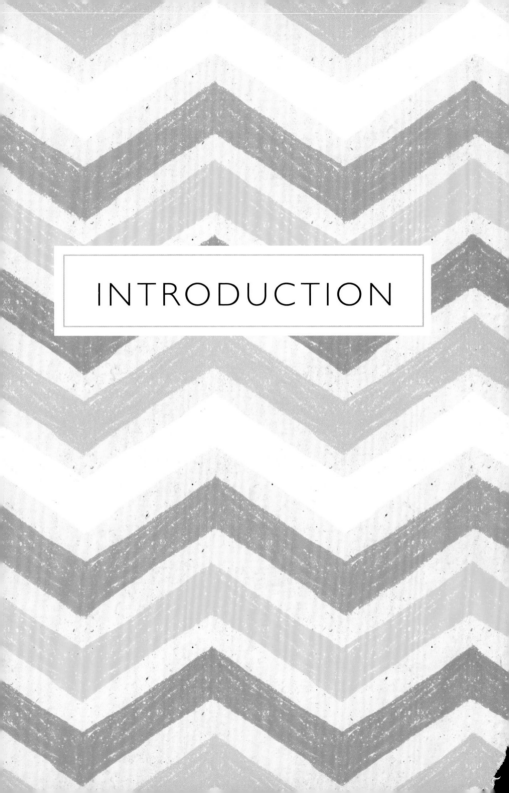

INTRODUCTION

Kind (adjective):

Having or showing a friendly, generous, and considerate nature.

"He thanked them for their kind and supportive actions."

Kindness doesn't have to involve a radical overhaul of your life. You don't need to sell all your worldly goods and go overseas to dedicate your life to a worthy cause, just the smallest acts of kindness that you can easily weave into your everyday life can make a real difference. That little compliment given to a colleague, words of appreciation for your partner, encouraging a friend in need, or making an effort for a stranger can all turn around someone's day for the better. Sometimes it's the smallest things that mean the most.

How to Live a Kind Life brings you ideas on how you can make kindness a daily habit, with suggestions for random acts of kindness along with inspiring quotes to motivate you to be more compassionate. In being kinder to others, not only do we help to build up trust, community, and empathy within society, we increase our own happiness levels. Kindness is reciprocal, so what we give we will one day get back in return. Furthermore, research has shown that altruistic behavior releases endorphins in the brain and therefore boosts our own feelings of well-being.

When dedicating to being kind to others, it's important not to miss out one incredibly important person…you. You know the saying "to love others, you must first love yourself" and the same goes for kindness. In order to be able to be genuinely kind to others, you need to first be kind to yourself. Self-care is an incredibly important aspect of forging and maintaining a life filled with kind acts.

Just one kind act a day has the power to turn a life around, so use this book as your guide, inspiration, and motivation to embrace a year of kind living.

"Be kind, for everyone you meet is fighting a hard battle."

– PLATO

"One kind word can warm three winter months."

– JAPANESE PROVERB

PAY FOR A STRANGER

Today if you're in a store, or buying a coffee, pay for the person behind you. Be sure to keep the gesture an anonymous one, perhaps with a cheery "have a good day!" message that you could ask the person behind the counter to convey to your lucky recipient.

"If you want others to be happy, practise compassion. If you want to be happy, practise compassion."

– DALAI LAMA

"Don't wait for people
to be friendly,
show them how."

– UNKNOWN

EAT WELL

One of the simplest ways to be kind to yourself is to eat well. Be conscious of what you consume and your body will thank you for it.

"Be kinder to yourself. And then let your kindness flood the world."

– PEMA CHODRON

"Those who bring sunshine to the lives of others cannot keep it from themselves."

– J.M. BARRIE

LET THEM KNOW YOU CARE

Write your partner a list of things you love about them. Whilst it may feel overly slushy, this kind of positive reinforcement is incredibly good for your relationship. It'll serve as a reminder to you of why you love them as well as making them feel all warm and fuzzy inside!

"There is nothing more truly artistic than to love people."

– VINCENT VAN GOGH

"A good character is the best tombstone. Those who loved you and were helped by you will remember you when forget-me-nots have withered. Carve your name on hearts, not on marble."

– CHARLES H. SPURGEON

BE POLITE

Hold the door open for the person behind you, let someone go in front of you in a line…small gestures such as these add up to create an enveloping attitude of kindness.

"Life's most persistent and nagging question is 'What are you doing for others?'"

– MARTIN LUTHER KING JR.

"How beautiful
a day can be,
when kindness
touches it!"

– GEORGE ELLISTON

"Kind words are short and easy to speak, but their echoes are truly endless."

– MOTHER TERESA

MEET FACE-TO-FACE

Instead of automatically texting or emailing, take time to connect
with people on a face-to-face level. Give your time over to them fully,
be genuinely attentive instead of squeezing them in and rushing off
because you're in a hurry.

DO NOT COMPARE YOURSELF TO OTHERS

People who are truly kind to themselves never compare themselves to others. We are all on our own journey, fighting our own battles, with our own individual set of strengths and weaknesses. We are all good at different things and we all have different ambitions, motivations, and priorities in life.

"If your compassion does
not include yourself,
it is incomplete. "

– JACK KORNFIELD

"There is no exercise better for the heart than reaching down and lifting people up."

– JOHN HOLMES

SAY SORRY

…You know who to. Don't hold onto grudges or petty resentments. Let them go and feel lighter in the process.

"Those best parts of a good life: little, nameless, unremembered acts of kindness and love."

– WILLIAM WORDSWORTH

"Too often we underestimate the power of a touch, a smile, a kind word, a listening ear, an honest compliment, or the smallest act of caring, all of which have the potential to turn a life around."

– LEO BUSCAGLIA

PRAISE A COLLEAGUE

Praise someone at work for a job well done. Try to do this when there
are other people around to hear — extra points if you can do this in
front of his/her boss!

"Perhaps you will forget tomorrow the kind words you say today, but the recipient may cherish them over a lifetime."

– DALE CARNEGIE

"Kindness is the twin sister of joy — we cannot have one without the other."

– HEATHER SHORE

"Three things in human life are important: the first is to be kind; the second is to be kind; and the third is to be kind."

– HENRY JAMES

"Be kind to unkind people – they need it the most."

– ASHLEIGH BRILLIANT

MAKE YOUR OWN MANTRAS

Write a list of life-affirming, positive statements to repeat to yourself whenever you are feeling inadequate or in need of a boost. You can adapt these to your own personal preferences and circumstances, but affirmations such as "I am enough," "I deserve happiness," and "I am worthy of all the kindness that comes my way" may be useful starting points.

"If the words you spoke appeared on your skin, would you still be beautiful?"

– AULIQ ICE

CARVE OUT TIME FOR YOURSELF

Every day make sure you take time out for yourself to do something
that brings you joy, whether it's a craft, a hobby, painting, reading,
or just sitting in peace for five minutes.

"Give yourself some kindness today until you're filled and pass it on."

– LORI HIL

"Be kind to others,
so that you may learn the
secret art of being kind
to yourself."

– PARAMAHANSA YOGANANDA

"If in our daily life we can smile, if we can be peaceful and happy, not only we, but everyone will profit from it. This is the most basic kind of peace work."

– THICH NHAT HANH

"The words of kindness
are more healing to a
drooping heart than balm
or honey."

– SARAH FIELDING

GIVE A STRANGER
A GIFT

Leave a gift for someone in a random public place. It's a good idea to drop this in a spot where people actually stop and sit, such as a bus stop or in a café, so people don't just hurriedly walk past oblivious to your offering.

DON'T JUDGE

The more you judge others, the more harshly you tend to judge
yourself, so nobody wins from taking this particular standpoint in life.
Remember you don't know other people's stories and battles, and you're
in no position to judge anyway.

"Through lovingkindness, everyone and everything can flower again from within."

– SHARON SALZBERG

"When you are kind to someone in trouble, you hope they'll remember and be kind to someone else. And it'll become like a wildfire."

– WHOOPI GOLDBERG

FORGIVE YOURSELF

We all make mistakes. Instead of dwelling on them, just resolve to do better in the future and move on.

"Do not speak badly of yourself. For the Warrior within hears your words and is lessened by them."

– DAVID GEMMELL

"And in spite of the fancies of youth, there's nothing so kingly as kindness, and nothing so royal as truth."

– ALICE CARY

STAND UP FOR SOMEONE

If someone in a vulnerable position is being bullied or talked down to, stand up for them. Speak out and protect them from unkind words or actions.

"A kind and compassionate act is often its own reward."

– WILLIAM JOHN BENNETT

SHARE

Very different from giving away things you no longer need, sharing
is about giving away a little of something that is meaningful to you,
whether it be half of your lunch, your favorite dress you could loan to
a friend for a special occasion, or even words of advice.

"When you are kind
to others, it not only changes
you, it changes the world."

– HAROLD KUSHNER

"One of the most difficult things to give away is kindness; it usually comes back to you."

- UNKNOWN

TREAT YOURSELF

If you get a promotion at work, meet a deadline, do something around the house that's been on your to-do list for ages…treat yourself. However minor your accomplishment may seem, treat yourself — whether in the form of a slice of cake, an item of clothing you've been coveting, or a coffee with a friend. Whatever makes you happy and positively reinforces your actions.

"The first rule of
kindness is to be kind
to yourself."

- BRYANT MCGILL

COMMENT ON
A BLOG

If you have enjoyed reading a blog, leave a positive comment.

"For beautiful eyes, look for the good in others; for beautiful lips, speak only words of kindness; and for poise, walk with the knowledge that you are never alone."

– AUDREY HEPBURN

"Compassion isn't about solutions.
It's about giving all the love that
you've got."

– CHERYL STRAYED,
TINY BEAUTIFUL THINGS

"If we all do one random act of kindness daily, we might just set the world in the right direction."

– MARTIN KORNFELD

EMBRACE THE GOOD

Studies have shown that we subconsciously self-sabotage what we think we don't deserve, so if you don't think you are worthy of good things you won't accept them into your life. Tell yourself each day that you deserve all the positivity that comes your way. Be kind to yourself by embracing the good stuff.

"You can't live a perfect day without doing something for someone who will never be able to repay you."

– JOHN WOODEN

THE GIFT OF MUSIC

Make a playlist for a friend who needs cheering up. They'll know you've put time, effort, and thought into this and that knowledge will make them smile every time they listen to it.

"Kindness is the language which the deaf can hear and the blind can see."

– MARK TWAIN

"If your words are soft and sweet, they won't be as hard to swallow if you have to eat them."

– UNKNOWN

PARK AND WALK

Park at the opposite end of the parking lot from the store, that way you'll give yourself some exercise as well as leaving nearer spaces free for those who may really need them.

"No act of kindness, no matter how small, is ever wasted."

– AESOP

"Kindness in words creates confidence. Kindness in thinking creates profoundness. Kindness in giving creates love."

– LAO TZU

COMPLIMENT

Make the effort to genuinely compliment at least three people —
today and every day. Focus on things as trivial as a new haircut,
through to character traits and achievements.

"Kindness is not a business.
True kindness expects
nothing in return and should
never act with conditions."

– RAY T. BENNETT

"The dew of compassion
is a tear."

– LORD BYRON

"One can pay back the loan of gold, but one dies forever in debt to those who are kind."

– MALAYAN PROVERB

EXPRESS YOUR LOVE

Try saying "I love you" to friends and family a little more often.

"What wisdom can you find that is greater than kindness?"

– JEAN-JACQUES ROUSSEAU

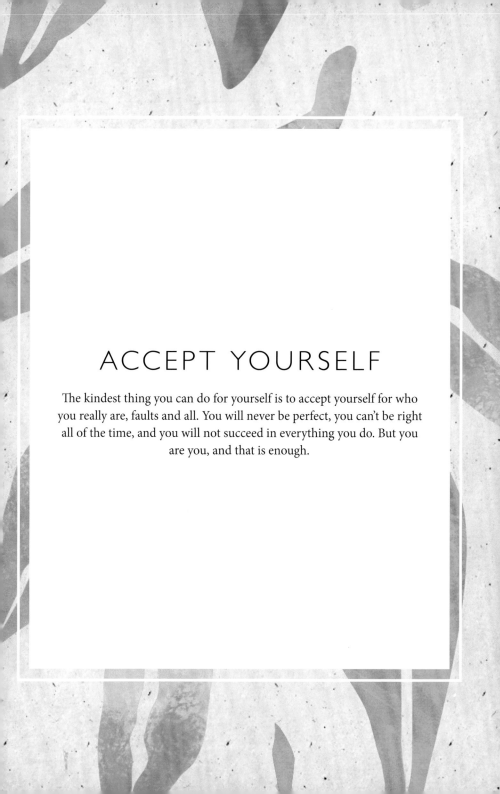

ACCEPT YOURSELF

The kindest thing you can do for yourself is to accept yourself for who you really are, faults and all. You will never be perfect, you can't be right all of the time, and you will not succeed in everything you do. But you are you, and that is enough.

"Be gentle first with yourself if you wish to be gentle with others."

– LAMA YESHE

"There is nothing more beautiful than someone who goes out of their way to make life beautiful for others."

– MANDY HALE

"It's cool to be kind."

– UNKNOWN

ADOPT A PET

Visit your local dog or cat rescue center and adopt an animal in need.
Your kindness will be paid back tenfold by the love and joy a pet will
bring into your life.

"It is the characteristic of the magnanimous man to ask no favor but to be ready to do kindness to others."

– ARISTOTLE

"We rise by
lifting others."

– ROBERT INGERSOLL

EXPRESS YOUR GRATITUDE

Perhaps someone working in a store or restaurant has been really helpful to you, or maybe they have a really great manner with the public. Instead of just thinking it, tell them. Even small expressions of gratitude can make someone's day.

SPARE CHANGE?

Why not tape it to a parking meter for the next person.

"We don't have to engage in grand, heroic actions to participate in the process of change. Small acts, when multiplied by millions of people, can transform the world."

– HOWARD ZINN

PLAN A STREET PARTY

This is a great way to do something for a number of people at the same time. It's a way of including more isolated neighbors, introducing people, and creating a happy community environment. Neighbors young and old will enjoy the chance to celebrate and socialize with one another.

"Kindness is doing what
you can, where you are,
with what you have."

– UNKNOWN

"Self-compassion is simply giving the same kindness to ourselves that we would give to others."

– CHRISTOPHER GERMER

DATE YOURSELF

Be kind to you. Take yourself off on a date to the theater, out for a meal, or treat yourself to a spa day.

"When a woman becomes her own best friend life is easier."

— DIANE VON FURSTENBERG

"Kindness is like snow — it beautifies everything it covers."

– KAHLIL GIBRAN

"A tree is known by its fruit; a man by his deeds. A good deed is never lost; he who sows courtesy reaps friendship, and he who plants kindness gathers love."

– SAINT BASIL

DO SOMEONE'S SHOPPING

Offer to shop for a homebound friend or neighbor. A little goes a long way for people unable to leave the house and be as agile and independent as they would like to be.

"A warm smile is the universal language of kindness."

– WILLIAM ARTHUR WARD

"Goodness is about character – integrity, honesty, kindness, generosity, moral courage, and the like. More than anything else, it is about how we treat other people."

– DENNIS PRAGER

SEND POSTCARDS

Find postcards with appropriate pictures on for various friends and drop them a random note just to thank them for being such a good friend.

"Forget injuries; never forget kindness."

– CONFUCIUS

"Do all the good you can.
By all the means you can. In all the
ways you can. In all the places you
can. At all the times you can. To all
the people you can. As long as ever
you can."

– JOHN WESLEY

"The smallest act of kindness is worth more than the grandest intention."

– OSCAR WILDE

"Every sunrise is an invitation for us to arise and brighten someone's day."

– RICHELLE E. GOODRICH

"By a sweet tongue and kindness, you can drag an elephant with a hair."

– PERSIAN PROVERB

"The way you speak to others can offer them joy, happiness, self-confidence, hope, trust, and enlightenment."

– THICH NHAT HANH

STOP COMPLAINING

Try to go a whole week without complaining about anything, and note the effect it has both on you and the people surrounding you. It will be more difficult than you think, but also more rewarding than you ever thought possible.

"It's easy to hate, it takes strength to be gentle and kind."

– THE SMITHS

VOLUNTEER

Volunteer to help others in need, perhaps at a homeless shelter serving meals or find an organization that matches your concerns and passions.

"If those who owe us nothing gave us nothing, how poor we would be."

– ANTONIO PORCHIA

"Those who make compassion an essential part of their lives find the joy of life. Kindness deepens the spirit and produces rewards that cannot be completely explained in words."

– ROBERT J. FUREY

GIVE BLOOD

You could be helping someone in a life-threatening situation.

"How do we change the world? One random act of kindness at a time."

– MORGAN FREEMAN

QUIT THE CRITICAL SELF TALK

Your niggling inner voice can be your worst critic, undermining your achievements and belittling your character. As these critical thoughts arise, replace each one with a positive statement about yourself.

"Put down the bat
and pick up a feather,
give yourself a
break."

– UNKNOWN

HUG

Give more hugs! According to scientific research, hugging makes us healthier, happier, and more resilient.

"Get out of your head
and into your heart.
Think less.
Feel more."

– OSHO

"Kindness is more important than wisdom, and the recognition of this is the beginning of wisdom."

– THEODORE ISAAC RUBIN

"By swallowing evil words unsaid, no one has ever harmed his stomach."

– WINSTON CHURCHILL

"Be the person that makes others feel special. Be known for your kindness and grace."

– UNKNOWN

"Even when you are hurt
being kind to others will
help the hurt."

– CATHERINE PULSIFER

WISH THEM LUCK!

Buy a dozen lottery tickets and hand them out to strangers
on the street.

HAVE COMPASSION

If someone has done something you don't like or is being rude to you, instead of going on the defensive try to be compassionate toward their situation. Tell yourself maybe they're just having a bad day. Perhaps all they need is to hear a kind word from you and they'll do a U-turn on their attitude — you may be surprised at the results if you try this one!

"I have no desire to move mountains, construct monuments, or leave behind in my wake material evidence of my existence. But in the final recollection, if the essence of my being has caused a smile to have appeared upon your face or a touch of joy within your heart... then in living — I have made my mark."

– THOMAS L. ODEM, JR.

"One person can make a difference, and everyone should try."

– JOHN F. KENNEDY

"There are no traffic jams when you go the extra mile."

– KENNETH MCFARLAND

"We think too much and feel too little. More than machinery, we need humanity. More than cleverness, we need kindness and gentleness."

– CHARLIE CHAPLIN

MAKE THAT PHONE CALL

We all have people we haven't seen in a while who we keep meaning to call. Do it today and make their day. Whether it's a relative or an old friend, perhaps someone who moved jobs or out of your neighborhood, they will be pleased to hear from you.

LEND AN ELDERLY PERSON A HAND

Helping someone less agile than yourself across the road, or to reach something from a high shelf in the supermarket is no great effort for you but this simple act of kindness could really make a difference to someone else's day.

"Beginning today, treat everyone you meet as if they were going to be dead by midnight. Extend to them all the care, kindness and understanding you can muster, and do it with no thought of any reward. Your life will never be the same again."

– OG MANDINO